NAUVOO

NAUVOO

MORMON CITY ON THE MISSISSIPPI RIVER

RAYMOND BIAL

Houghton Mifflin Company

Boston 2006

www.houghtonmifflinbooks.com

The text of this book is set in Berkeley Book.
Illustrations on pages 8, 9, 10, 13, and 14
courtesy of Community of Christ Archives, Independence, Missouri.
All other photos by Raymond Bial.
Map by Jerry Malone.

Library of Congress Cataloging-in-Publication Data

Bial, Raymond.
Nauvoo : Mormon city on the Mississippi River / by Raymond Bial.
p. cm.
ISBN-13: 978-0-618-39685-6 (hardcover)
ISBN-10: 0-618-39685-3 (hardcover)
1. Church of Jesus Christ of Latter-day Saints—Illinois—
Nauvoo—History—19th century—Juvenile literature. 2. Nauvoo (Ill.)—
Church history—19th century—Juvenile literature. I. Title.
BX8615.I3B53 2006   289.3'77343—dc22   2005027528

Printed in Singapore
TWP 10 9 8 7 6 5 4 3 2 1

This book is dedicated to all the good people who have worked
to preserve and rebuild the community of Nauvoo.

I would like to thank the many people who helped in the research, writing,
and photography for this book, notably Nauvoo Restoration, Inc., Grant Anderson,
Steven L. Olsen, Russ Taylor, Ron Romig, and my editor, Erica Zappy.

This book is dedicated to all the good people who have worked
to preserve and rebuild the community of Nauvoo.

I would like to thank the many people who helped in the research, writing,
and photography for this book, notably Nauvoo Restoration, Inc., Grant Anderson,
Steven L. Olsen, Russ Taylor, Ron Romig, and my editor, Erica Zappy.

In early 1839, members of the religious group known as the Church of Jesus Christ of Latter-day Saints once again fled for their lives. Climbing onto wooden ferries, men, women, and children hurried across the Mississippi River from the state of Missouri to safety in Illinois.

The Mormons, as church members are known, had been persecuted from the very start. Their religion began in 1820 when a young man named Joseph Smith had a revelation near Palmyra, New York. Joseph later said, "Two personages whose brightness and glory defy all description" appeared before him. "One of them spake unto me . . . and said, pointing to the other: This is my Beloved Son. Hear Him."

The word *Mormon* came from another revelation of Joseph Smith's, occurring in 1823 when he was seventeen, in which an angel called Moroni appeared before him. The angel led Joseph to several hidden golden plates inscribed in "reformed Egyptian" hieroglyphics and a set of "seer stones" that enabled the young man to read the plates. In revelations from 1823 to 1827, the angel told Joseph that he was to translate these plates. Joseph then published his translation of the engravings on the plates as the Book of Mormon.

This book recounts the story of ancient Hebrew peoples who migrated to North America long before the arrival of Columbus. The first people were said to be the Jaredites of the House of Israel who left the Tower of Babel. The book tells how they were swept

across the Pacific Ocean in extraordinary barges to the west coast of Central America. These people created magnificent cities and civilizations in North America, but eventually destroyed themselves. Leaving Jerusalem around 600 B.C., Father Lehi and his family, including Laman, Lemuel, and Nephi, migrated to America and inherited the land of the Jaredites. The Book of Mormon claims that Jesus Christ visited these people upon his ascension to heaven, bringing the Christian message to the Continent. Yet conflicts between the three brothers, Nephi on one side and Laman and Lemuel on the other, led to two factions: the Nephites and Lamanites. Wars between these two groups ultimately destroyed the Nephites, leaving only Moroni, who completed the golden plates, written by his father Mormon. The angel then buried the golden plates between the year 400 and 421 near Joseph Smith's home in New York. After Joseph completed his translation, it is believed that the angel swept the golden plates away.

Opposite page: *Joseph Smith (1805–1844), founder of the Church of Jesus Christ of Latter-Day Saints.*
Top, left: *Emma Smith with her son David Hyrum, born November 1844, five months after the murder of Joseph Smith.*
Top, right: *Lucy Mack Smith (1775–1856), mother of Joseph, lived in Nauvoo—until her death at the age of eighty.*

The Book of Mormon came to be viewed not as the Mormon Bible but as a supplement to the King James version of the Christian Bible. The Mormons grew to believe that God revealed many "great and important things" on various occasions. Divine revelations to Joseph were collected in Doctrine and Covenants, and The Pearl of Great Price includes sayings attributed to Moses and Abraham. Joseph came to be thought of as a prophet, like those in the Old Testament, as did his eventual successor, Brigham Young. Mormons followed most traditional Christian beliefs, such as the existence of God, Christ as his son, and heaven and hell. Mormons baptized members, confirmed believers, and celebrated Holy Communion. Yet Mormons have long insisted that they are not Protestants. Members often refer to themselves as Latter-day Saints or simply as Saints.

The Church of Jesus Christ of Latter-day Saints (LDS), known as the Mormon church, would become one of the largest, most active churches in the United States. It now has more than ten million members and is still growing rapidly not only in America but throughout the world. Over the years, Mormons have come to be accepted, but that was not the case when Joseph Smith and five others founded the church on April 6, 1830, in New York State.

In establishing the Mormon Church, Joseph claimed that he was a prophet who directly spoke with God. He believed that the end of the world was near and that Mormons had a duty to found a society called a "New Zion." Here the believers would gather and provide a proper place for the Messiah upon his return. Subjected to ridicule and persecution in New York, Joseph led the Mormons to Kirtland, Ohio, near Cleveland, in 1831. In Ohio, they built a community that would become their New Zion. Their community flourished, and the group continued to grow rapidly. Begun in 1833 and dedicated in 1836, members of the new religion built a magnificent temple, which served as a place for worship and instruction.

As in the Old Testament, Mormons had leaders called patriarchs and buildings called temples, along with pastors and meetinghouses. Through divine revelation, the Mormons restored sacred, ancient temple rituals that gave spiritual power to worthy people. The Latter-day Saints believed that they were the "chosen people," which appealed to many. Whole Protestant congregations converted to the new religion.

Yet others raged against the Mormons and their beliefs. Like other denominations, the Mormons sought religious freedom in the United States. Still the Mormons came to be persecuted—just as Catholics, Shakers, the Amish, and other groups at one time faced intolerance because of their beliefs. Their Christian neighbors in Ohio objected to the

Opposite page: *Brigham Young (1801–1877) led the Mormon Exodus of 1846, following the death of Joseph Smith.*
Above: *The Nauvoo Temple was rebuilt on the original site on a bluff overlooking the city and the Mississippi River.*

Mormons' claim that they were a chosen people. People resented the prosperity of the hard-working Mormons. The Mormons tried to keep to themselves in their private enclave, but they were soon driven from Ohio because of hostility and hatred.

Some of Joseph's closest followers also objected to some beliefs and abandoned him at Kirtland. Earlier, in 1831, Joseph and his wife, Emma, had lost twin babies at birth. This tragedy, along with threats from neighbors and conflicts within the church, might have broken a weaker person than Joseph Smith. Yet he remained a powerful and determined man. Moreover, he was blessed with a strong wife and a loving family that included Julia, Joseph III, Frederick, and later Alexander, who was born in 1838 in Far West, Missouri. Joseph's mother, Lucy Mack Smith, said of Emma, "I have never seen a woman in my life,

Above: Joseph Smith and his family moved into this cabin in 1839 and lived here until the Nauvoo Mansion was built.
Opposite page: The Mormons were attacked and driven from their Missouri homes, which were burned to the ground.

who would endure every specie of fatigue and hardship, from month to month, and from year to year with that unflinching courage, zeal, and patience, which she has done."

Joseph Smith decided that the Mormons had to move again—this time to Missouri where a Mormon settlement already existed. Like so many other American settlers, he had a dream that the Saints might find peace and prosperity in the West. Despite the early struggles of the new religion, many people continued to be drawn to the charismatic leader. His loyal friend Parley Pratt said Joseph "was in person tall and well built, strong and active; of a light complexion, light hair, blue eyes, very little beard, and an expression peculiar to himself, on which the eye naturally rested with interest, and was never weary of beholding." He further described Joseph as intelligent, cheerful, and down to earth. Joseph enjoyed athletics, such as good-natured wrestling matches, as well as preaching about his new religion. When Joseph declared that the Mormons should move again, many of the Saints followed him.

Governor Lilburn Boggs tolerated the Mormons who began to move to Missouri—at first. He even set aside territory in the north-central part of the state, where the Mormons could hopefully live in peace. Church members settled at the community of Independence over several years. However, other settlers in the region soon clashed with the Saints. Like

their opponents in Ohio, some people in Missouri resented Mormon claims that they were a "chosen people." Mormon opposition to slavery especially angered some Missouri settlers. So many Mormons poured into the territory that other settlers felt overwhelmed.

Threatened with violence, the Mormons fled to the community of Far West, Missouri, but conflicts intensified, especially when the Mormons now decided to defend themselves. At a Fourth of July gathering in 1838, the church elder Sidney Rigdon declared, "We will never be the aggressors, we will infringe on the rights of no people; but shall stand for our own until death. . . . No one shall be at liberty to come into our streets, to threaten us with mobs, for if he does, he shall atone for it before he leaves the place."

Attacks on their settlements soon led to the Missouri Mormon War. As mobs burned their cabins, the Mormons fought back, although they were hopelessly outnumbered. On October 27, 1838, Governor Boggs issued what became known as the "Extermination Order." In this statement, the governor declared, "The Mormons must be treated as enemies and must be exterminated or driven from the state." The governor's words provoked further attacks on the Mormons. In one horrifying episode, a mob murdered eighteen men and boys who had hidden in a blacksmith shop.

Soldiers then surrounded the Far West settlement and captured Joseph Smith. Government officials accused Joseph of treason and decided to execute him by firing squad. However, an honorable officer refused to carry out this unlawful order. Joseph Smith was then unjustly imprisoned at Liberty, Missouri. Without their leader, the Mormons faced a frightening crisis.

At this time, a First Presidency of three men led the church: Joseph Smith and two counselors. Just below the presidency was a group of church leaders called the Quorum of the Twelve Apostles. Modeled after Christ's disciples, the Twelve Apostles spread Mormon beliefs throughout the world and helped to lead the Saints. At this time, Brigham Young

was the senior member of this group. Brigham and the other Apostles helped the Mormons to escape Missouri before their homes were destroyed and their men, women, and children were hunted down and killed. After he and his family were forced to abandon Far West, Anson Call remembered, "My children nearly froze to death. . . . They killed our cattle, stole our horses."

Parley Pratt later wrote, "On the 17th of March, 1839, my wife took leave of the prison with her little children, and, with a broken heart returned to Far West, Missouri . . . the middle of April a gang of robbers entered Far West armed, and ordered my wife . . . and the others to be gone . . . or they would murder them. This gang destroyed much furniture and other property."

Opposite page: *Missouri governor Lilburn W. Boggs issued an order to exterminate the Mormons or drive them out of the state.* Above: *As they fled across the Mississippi River, the Mormons hoped for a better life in the Illinois city of Nauvoo.*

Cold, bedraggled, and terrified, the Mormons trudged east to the Mississippi River and escaped to Illinois in early 1839. The exiles were kindly welcomed in Quincy and other towns along both the Iowa and Illinois sides of the river. Shopkeepers and craftsmen in these communities respected the Mormons as good, hard-working people. The Saints also brought more trade to these villages and towns. Politicians realized that the Mormons might also be encouraged to vote for their candidates in elections.

Joseph Smith decided that the Mormons had to make the most of this goodwill. As he was being moved to another Missouri jail, a sympathetic guard encouraged the Mormon leader to escape custody and flee across the Mississippi River to Illinois. On the banks of

Above: *Located in the Old Nauvoo Burial Grounds, this bronze statue commemorates early Mormon pioneers.*
Opposite page: *The layout of streets and locations of some of the homes and businesses of Nauvoo.*

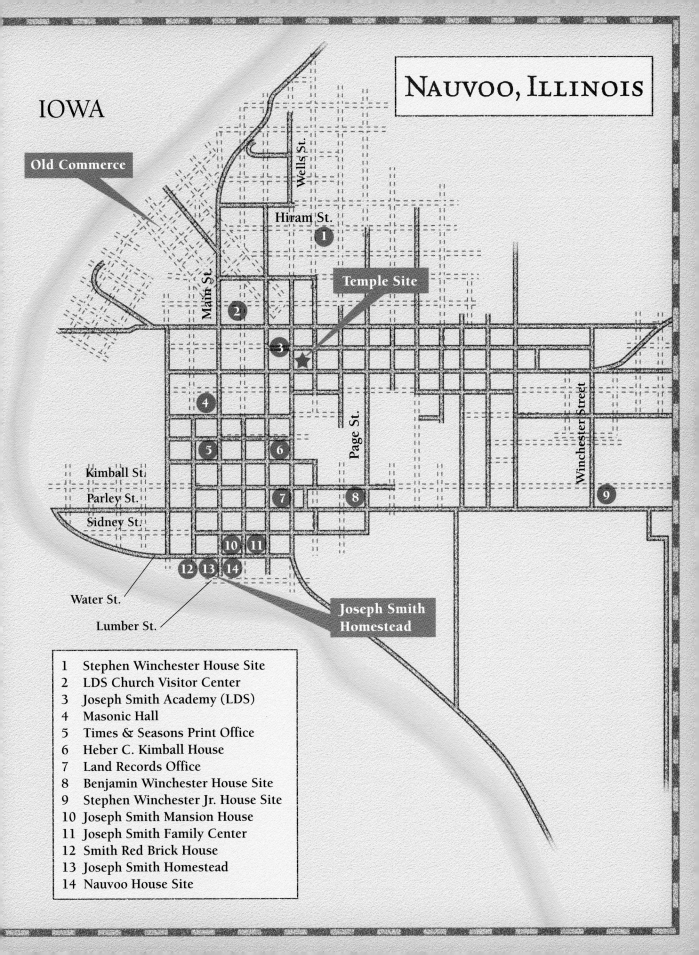

NAUVOO, ILLINOIS

IOWA

Old Commerce

Wells St.

Hiram St.

1

Temple Site

Main St.

2

3

Page St.

Winchester Street

4

5

6

Kimball St.

Parley St.

7

8

9

Sidney St.

10 11

12 13 14

Water St.

Lumber St.

Joseph Smith
Homestead

1   Stephen Winchester House Site
2   LDS Church Visitor Center
3   Joseph Smith Academy (LDS)
4   Masonic Hall
5   Times & Seasons Print Office
6   Heber C. Kimball House
7   Land Records Office
8   Benjamin Winchester House Site
9   Stephen Winchester Jr. House Site
10 Joseph Smith Mansion House
11 Joseph Smith Family Center
12 Smith Red Brick House
13 Joseph Smith Homestead
14 Nauvoo House Site

this broad river, Joseph decided to build another city to be called Nauvoo from a Hebrew word meaning "the city beautiful."

Originally the Sac and Fox Indians had inhabited this region, which they called Quashquema, a Fox word meaning "peaceful place." As American settlers pushed westward, Captain James White established a fur-trading post along the riverbank. A village that soon came to be known as Commerce grew around the trading post. The collection of humble log cabins was situated on the high ground, simply called the Hill, facing the Mississippi River. The low ground, or "flats," between Commerce and the river was regarded as useless swamp. It was not worth the labor of cultivation, especially when plenty of cheap high ground was available. People who settled on the wet ground also became weak and feverish with ague, or malaria, which was carried by mosquitoes.

When Joseph and the Latter-day Saints arrived in Commerce they wished to freely practice their religion and safely raise their families. As Joseph and his family settled into a small cabin, he expressed his hope that he and his friends would there "find a resting place for a little season at least." Joseph further noted, "The conduct of the Saints, under their accumulated wrongs and sufferings, has been praiseworthy; their courage in defending their brethren from the ravages of the mobs; their attachment to the cause of truth, under circumstances the most trying and distressing which humanity can possibly endure; their love to each other, their readiness to afford assistance to me and my brethren who were confined in a dungeon; their sacrifice in leaving Missouri, and assisting the poor widows and orphans, and securing them houses in a more hospitable land; all conspire to raise them in the estimation of all good and virtuous men."

However, when the Mormons arrived in Nauvoo, they were impoverished. Conflicts were also growing within the church, as people faced the daunting task of starting over yet again. At this critical moment, Joseph Smith made a bold decision. Instead of calling upon his strongest leaders to build a new community, he sent them as missionaries to other parts of the United States and Great Britain.

Opposite page: *Facing west, the Joseph Smith homestead overlooked the Mississippi River.*
Above: *The Mormons purchased tools, nails, and other supplies for building homes at the mercantile on Main Street.*

Under the leadership of Brigham Young, these missionaries converted thousands of new members who journeyed to Nauvoo to make new homes for themselves and their families.

During the Industrial Revolution, many people in Great Britain had moved to cities, where they endured miserable lives. They worked long hours in factories yet barely survived in overcrowded slums built in the shadows of towering smokestacks. The new Mormon religion gave hope to these people. In 1840, the first British immigrants started to arrive in Nauvoo. Like so many other immigrants to the United States, the Mormon converts longed for a better life. They also brought great skills and intelligence, which would soon strengthen the growing community of Nauvoo.

Joseph Smith realized that he needed substantial land for all the Mormons who had journeyed from Missouri and for the many converts arriving every day. So he bought large parcels of land on both sides of the wide river on credit, mostly the unwanted and uncultivated bottom ground that lay between Commerce and the Mississippi River. He then sold lots to the converts as they arrived in Nauvoo. Upon returning from a mission in Great Britain, Joseph Fielding noted, "Late in the evening . . . we came in sight of some neat cottages fenced with

Opposite page and above: *After arriving in Nauvoo, the Mormons constructed wood-frame homes, brick houses, and log cabins.*

pickets, manifesting to us that the hand of industry was there different from anything we have seen since leaving England, even by the light of the moon; this was the first we saw of the city of the Saints. . . . We soon passed the temple, went from street to street, as in some large city. . . . I can truly say that the place, in generation, exceeds my expectations."

To drain the marshy flats along the river, the Mormons designed and dug an intricate network of irrigation ditches. This massive project required careful planning and thousands of hours of labor, since water seeped from both the bluff and the riverbanks. However, the Mormons were accustomed to hard work, and the drainage system was so effective that it is still in use today. Joseph also planned a large canal to channel power from the flowing waters of the Mississippi River. He wrote in his journal, "Met in council in the old house, then walked down to the river to look at the stream, rocks . . . suggested the idea of petitioning Congress for a grant to make a canal over the falls, or a dam to turn the water to the city, so that we might erect mills and other machinery." However, the Mormons didn't have time to undertake this ambitious project. Joseph also hoped to build a large hotel to house all the visitors that he envisioned coming to the bustling city. Called

Nauvoo House, the hotel was to be located on the bank of the river, next to Joseph Smith's Homestead, at the end of Main Street. Nauvoo House was chartered and work began in 1841, but the hotel was never completed during Joseph's lifetime.

To prevent further persecution and violence, Joseph wanted the Saints to be in charge of the city government. Therefore, he sought a city charter for his people from the Illinois state legislature. Obtained in December 1840, this charter provided for city courts with judges elected by the Mormons and with juries chosen from the Mormon community. If mobs attacked the Mormons, they could then be brought to justice. Under the charter, the Mormons were also allowed to organize the Nauvoo legion, a militia of five thousand men, to defend the city. Joseph Smith was chosen as mayor and lieutenant-general of the militia. The government and militia strengthened Mormon defenses and helped Nauvoo become a prosperous city. This blend of religious, civic, and military power began to worry people in Illinois. Yet in a letter to the editor of the *Times and Seasons,* signed "An American," one person wrote, "Before taking my farewell of your beautiful and growing city, I avail myself of a few . . . moments in expressing some of my views and conclusions of the 'Prophet Joe' and the Mormons. . . . Before visiting the place, my mind was very much prejudiced against the Mormons . . . [however] there is not a city within my knowledge that can boast of a more enterprising and industrious people than Nauvoo. Her citizens are enlightened, and possess many advantages in the arts and sciences of the day."

Mormon missionaries continued to travel widely in search of converts for their new community. Many journeyed through the southern United States, while others went to Europe spreading the word about the new faith. Hundreds of converts continued to stream into Nauvoo. Carpenters were kept busy, as were workers in the brickyard who made thousands of red clay bricks by hand. By 1844, within three years of its founding, the city had a population of more than 12,000. By 1846, Nauvoo had grown into one of the largest cities in Illinois—as populous as Chicago at the time—and the tenth largest city in the United States.

Opposite page, top: *At the time of his death, Joseph Smith and his family were living in the Mansion House.*
Opposite page, bottom: *The building of the Nauvoo House was completed by Lewis Bidamon, Emma Smith's second husband.*

Joseph wrote, "So many of my friends and acquaintances arriving in one day kept me very busy receiving their congratulations and answering their questions. I was rejoiced to meet them in such good health and fine spirits; for they were equal to any that had ever come to Nauvoo."

Nauvoo became renowned for its lovely homes, stores, and workshops. A small kingdom tucked in the western corner of the state, the bustling city had about two thousand homes, mostly log cabins, but also two hundred or so red brick houses. As in other frontier homesteads, industrious families provided for themselves by planting gardens and raising livestock. They were skilled at many crafts: baking, quilting, and candle making. They made their own soap. They also carded and spun wool, which was woven into cloth.

Like other pioneer communities, Nauvoo had a number of shops in which artisans practiced their crafts and sold their products. Village craftsmen included a blacksmith, cooper, wheelwright, furniture maker, rope maker, and many others. At the Stoddard Tin Shop, candleholders and other household objects were shaped. At the Riser Boot Shop, people could have shoes and boots made by hand.

Above: *Jonathan Browning located his well-known gunsmith shop along the east side of Main Street.*
Opposite page: *Joseph Smith's Red Brick Store, built in 1841.*

One of the most notable businesses was the Jonathan Browning Home and Gunsmith Shop. A Kentucky native who became a Mormon in Quincy, Browning invented one of the earliest repeating rifles. In 1845, he established his shop and living quarters for his family in a brick building on Main Street. Here he crafted many of the weapons that the Mormons needed to defend themselves in Illinois. After Jonathan moved west with the Saints, his son Jonathan M. Browning invented and crafted many new firearms in Ogden, Utah, including the famous Browning automatic rifle.

Along Main Street, Nauvoo also had a post office and mercantile, which was stocked with frontier supplies ranging from sugar and coffee to nails and pottery. There was also a printing office, where two newspapers, *Times and Seasons* and the *Nauvoo Neighbor*, were published. The bustling community had other shops, such as Lyon Drug Store, where people could buy medicine, books, hardware, shoes, and other everyday necessities on the frontier. At Scovil Bakery there was a bustle oven in which Lucius and Lucy Scovil baked loaves of bread, tasty cakes, and gingerbread cookies to sell to the public. They also catered for socials at the Masonic Hall next door, where many cultural events took place.

Opened as a general store in 1842, Joseph Smith's Red Brick Store became the most prominent business in the community. Located near the river, it offered a variety of merchandise on the first floor. It also had an office for Bishop Newel K. Whitney, which served as the tithing office where people could donate money to the church. The second floor included Joseph Smith's office and church headquarters, along with a large council room, or "lodge room," where important matters were discussed. On March 17, 1842, the Relief Society was organized here, with Emma Smith chosen as president.

Mormon children attended Pendleton Log School in the back room of a log home on Kimball Street. People often gathered at the Cultural Hall for plays and other entertainment. At the Seventies Hall, there was a small chapel for worship and lectures. The first Nauvoo library was situated on the second floor. Missionaries often received instruction here before departing for distant lands. The Trail of Hope began at the Seventies Hall and continued to the Mississippi River, tracing the path of the Mormons who left Nauvoo and traveled west. Today, a wooden flatboat with a covered wagon, barrels, and wooden boxes recalls the 1846 exodus of these hardy pioneers.

The many houses in the community most significantly included Joseph Smith's homestead, a log cabin where the family lived from 1839 until the Mansion House was completed in 1843. The dwelling was then expanded to include a hotel wing. Within a few years, Joseph would depart from this home for the town of Carthage on what would become his last journey from home. The nearby family cemetery would become the final resting place for Joseph and Emma Smith, Hyrum Smith, Lucy Mack, and Joseph Smith, Sr.

In 1839, Theodore Turley erected the first new home built by a church member—a log cabin on a lot east of the Mansion House. Thereafter, many other new homes sprang up in Nauvoo. Using his excellent woodworking skills, Brigham Young built his own home in Nauvoo. The east wing of the house later served as headquarters and a meeting place for church leaders. John Taylor, the third president of the Church of Latter-day Saints, also had a home next to the *Times and Seasons* newspaper offices, where he served as editor in 1845. Joseph Smith's mother, Lucy Mack Smith, also lived in a two-story home, which was originally built in 1843 for the Joseph Noble family. The Mormons have since lovingly restored these and many other homes in honor of their founders.

After guiding the Mormons to Nauvoo, Joseph Smith planned to build a new temple, like the one in Kirtland, in which the Mormons could have sacred rituals. The impressive

Opposite page: *The back room of the Pendleton home served as a pioneer school.*
Above: *The home of Brigham Young, who became the second president of the Church of Jesus Christ of Latter-day Saints.*

Nauvoo Temple was to be constructed on a bluff—the highest spot for miles around Nauvoo. Overlooking the city and the river, the temple was to be the Mormon's most ambitious undertaking. Limestone for the building was cut from a nearby quarry. When completed, the towering edifice was to be one hundred and twenty-eight feet long and eighty-eight feet wide. Ornate decorative caps, called Sunstones, each weighing two and a half tons, were to be placed atop each of the thirty pillars. This crown jewel of Nauvoo was to have a tower that would rise eighty-two feet from the ground. Like the Kirkland temple, it had meeting rooms on the first two floors. However, the basement and top floor were to be reserved for sacred rituals.

Temple rituals included washing and anointing, baptism for the dead, endowments, and eternal marriages. Joseph taught that even those who had passed away could receive the Christian gospel and be saved, so church members were sometimes baptized for the dead. In rituals known as endowments a person was led through the temple in a Plan of Salvation to become more like Christ. An individual made devout promises to undertake good works, which he or she could not discuss outside the temple. Individuals usually went through endowment ceremonies before embarking on a mission or getting married. After their own endowments, Mormons can go through the temple again on behalf of the deceased.

In another temple ceremony, a husband and wife were "sealed," or bound together for eternity. This ritual became controversial when Joseph also began to teach that a man could have more than one wife in a "celestial marriage." Joseph believed that he was

Above: *Nauvoo's first library was located on the upper floor of the Seventies Hall.*
Opposite page: *The Mormons held worship services and lectures in the Seventies Hall.*

returning to the practice of the Old Testament in which leaders often had several wives. However, polygamy, or plural marriage, went against the moral beliefs of the time. As early as 1831, Joseph had believed in polygamy but foresaw widespread opposition—both within and outside the Mormon community. He did not explain the doctrine until 1843 in Nauvoo. Many Mormons accepted the practice; others became deeply troubled. Word got out about men having multiple wives, and people became outraged. Joseph also began to teach other controversial beliefs—that people were as eternal as God; that human intelligence had existed forever, and that humans could become like gods themselves.

As the Mormons flourished in Nauvoo, they again suffered contempt for their beliefs, especially about marriage and family life. People in neighboring communities also resented their prosperity, political power, and independence. Some people wrongly feared that the Mormons might even try to establish their own nation separate from the United States. While Joseph was dealing with rising hostility around Nauvoo, the Missouri government sought to bring him to trial again—on false charges of resisting their state militia and as

an accomplice in an attempted murder of Lilburn Boggs. Missouri officers came to Illinois to arrest Joseph. The Mormon leader then fled and hid out for much of 1842 and 1843.

Meanwhile, Illinois politicians and newspaper editors continued to turn against the Mormons. Thomas Sharp, a Whig politician and editor of the *Warsaw Signal,* became very angry when the Mormons switched their support from a Whig to a Democratic candidate. In his newspaper published in the town of Warsaw, a few miles from Nauvoo, he launched a hateful campaign against the Mormons. He wrote that "under the sacred garb of Christianity" the Mormons "perpetuate the most lawless and diabolical deeds that ever, in any age of the world, disgraced the human species." He further accused the Saints of theft, counterfeiting, and other crimes. Sharp so inflamed people in western Illinois that Joseph Smith's life was again in danger.

In June 1844, the Nauvoo city council shut down The *Nauvoo Expositor,* a newspaper that had been critical of Joseph Smith and the Mormons. One of its publishers, William Law, was an excommunicated Mormon who bitterly hated Joseph Smith. Law held secret

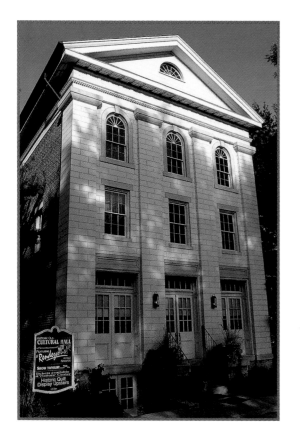

meetings in his home, in which he plotted the murder of the Mormon leader. Although the Mormons could legally close the press as a threat to the community, Joseph Smith, acting as mayor with the support of the city council, also ordered the sheriff to destroy the printing press, scatter the type, and burn any newspapers. These destructive acts inflamed many people in the region, convincing them that Joseph Smith had too much power. In the *Warsaw Signal,* Sharp urged violence against the Mormons: "Citizens arise, one and all!!! Can you stand by, and suffer such infernal devils to rob men of their property rights, without avenging them. We have no time for comment! Everyman will make his own. Let it be with powder and ball!"

Illinois governor Thomas Ford had once been friendly toward the Mormons, but he now turned against them. In his letters to Joseph, he came to make unfair demands against the Mormons. After reading one such letter, Joseph's brother Hyrum replied, "There is no mercy—no mercy here. No, just as sure as we fall into their hands we are dead men." Again fearing for his life, Joseph Smith crossed the Mississippi River, thinking that he might lead the Mormons to a safe place in the West, far away from the angry mobs. But then Joseph heard that his followers thought that he was abandoning them. "If my life is of no value to my friends, it is of none to myself," he observed. Joseph asked Hyrum for his advice and his brother said, "Let us go back and give ourselves up, and see this thing out." Joseph thought deeply, then he said, "If you go back I will go with you, but we shall be butchered."

Opposite page: *The Cultural Hall was used for church meetings, plays, concerts, funerals, and court sessions.*
Above: *Many businesses, including the Printing Office and the Post Office and Mercantile, were located on Main Street.*

Although fearing they would be murdered, Joseph and Hyrum returned to Nauvoo. In 1844, the two brothers and several of their friends were taken to jail for questioning in Carthage, Illinois, the county seat of Hancock County, twenty-four miles southeast of Nauvoo. Having a premonition of his fate, Joseph told his followers that he knew he would never return to Nauvoo—that he would be murdered. On June 18, 1844, he said, "Greater love hath no man than that he should lay down his life for his friends. You have stood by me in the hour of trouble, and I am willing to sacrifice my life for your preservation."

Afraid there would be a riot, Governor Ford came to Carthage to assure Joseph of his safety. He said that Joseph and his brother were guaranteed "protective custody" in the city jail. But then, abandoning Joseph, Hyrum, and their friends, the governor went to Nauvoo to search for a counterfeiting operation and to admonish the Mormons to obey the law. On June 27, 1844, a drunken mob of about a hundred men stormed the jail. They wildly fired gunshots as they broke into the second-floor room where Joseph, Hyrum, and their companions were being held. One of the thugs fired a bullet through the wooden door and murdered Hyrum Smith, who was trying to hold the attackers back. Another Mormon was wounded. Joseph Smith tried to escape through a window, but he was killed by gunfire

from thugs outside in the yard and others bursting into the room.

Governor Ford, who had failed miserably in protecting the Smiths, now feared that the Mormons would seek to avenge the brutal murders. However, the Mormons peacefully mourned the death of their leader and his brother. The bodies of Joseph and Hyrum Smith were brought back to Nauvoo. People were shocked that the man who had over the years escaped so many threats on his life had now been murdered. The bodies of the two brothers were secretly buried in the basement of the unfinished Nauvoo House; then later moved to the family cemetery on the Smith homestead across the street.

News of Joseph's death quickly spread to other Mormon communities throughout the United States. All the missionaries, including the Twelve Apostles, returned to Nauvoo. They attempted to protect the Mormons in Nauvoo and pondered who would succeed Joseph as their leader. On some occasions, Joseph had spoken as if his son would become head of the Mormons. At other times, he told the Twelve Apostles that they would lead the church. Brigham Young and others agreed that the Twelve Apostles should assume leadership. However, Sidney Rigdon, a close friend of Joseph's, thought that he should become the leader. William Smith, another brother of

Opposite page, left: *Statue of Joseph and Hyrum Smith.*
Opposite page, right: *Carthage Jail, where the brothers were murdered in 1844.*
Above, top: *With the bullet hole clearly visible, this is the door through which Hyrum Smith was shot and killed.*
Above, bottom: *Window in the upstairs room of the Carthage Jail, through which Joseph Smith was shot and killed.*

Joseph's, thought that he should head the church. Both men had some followers, but most Mormons accepted Brigham Young as their leader. He became the new Prophet and leader of the Church of Jesus Christ of Latter-day Saints. However, some Mormons did not support him or any of these men as their leader, and when the Mormons later moved to Utah, they quietly remained in the Midwest, some in Nauvoo. In 1860, these scattered people formed the Reorganized Church of Latter-day Saints (RLDS). They asked Joseph Smith's son, Joseph Smith III, to be their leader and prophet. Joseph's wife, Emma, stayed in Nauvoo, remarried, and joined this new church.

Joseph Smith's murderers were never brought to justice. Of the sixty suspects, nine men were tried, but none were ever convicted. Not only did these men go unpunished, but within a year after Joseph Smith's death, the persecution of the Mormons still raged throughout western Illinois. Soon after the trial, a mob attacked a Mormon settlement near Nauvoo, torching two hundred homes and barns and destroying farm crops. A mob then drove the sheriff out of Carthage because he was sympathetic to the plight of the Mormons. In response, the sheriff deputized a Mormon posse to take back the town.

Fearing more violence, the governor urged Brigham Young to lead the Mormons out of Nauvoo. If they did not, the governor warned that the Mormons would be forcibly removed. Citizen committees from Hancock and Adams counties also demanded that the Mormons had to abandon Nauvoo. Some people decided to stay, but the overwhelming majority followed Brigham Young west to fulfill a vision related to him by Joseph Smith.

Above: The graves of Hyrum, Joseph, and Emma near the Smith Homestead along the east bank of the Mississippi River. Opposite page: The table in Brigham Young's home where Mormon leaders decided to leave Nauvoo and move west.

In the seven years they had lived and worked in Nauvoo, the Mormons had built impressive brick homes and businesses, which would now have to be abandoned along with many of their household goods. Surrounded by hostile people, the Mormons had to flee as soon as possible. No one would buy Mormon property, since they knew it would soon be left behind and the local people could have about two million dollars' worth of houses, buildings, and land—for nothing. Bathseba Smith recalled, "My last act in that precious spot was to tidy the rooms, sweep up the floor, and set the broom in its accustomed place behind the door. Then with emotions in my heart . . . I gently closed that door and faced an unknown future."

In the midst of this turmoil, the Mormons worked desperately to fulfill a promise to complete the temple before they departed from Nauvoo. For protection, the workers brought their guns along with their tools, and guards kept watch. Despite the constant fear of attack, Brigham Young reported, "The Temple has progressed very rapidly since the death of our beloved Prophet and Patriarch. . . .We wish all the young, middle aged, and able bodied men who have it in their hearts to stretch forth this work with power, to come to Nauvoo, prepared to stay during the summer, and to bring with them means to sustain

themselves with, and to enable us to forward this work." On December 10, 1845, the temple was nearly finished and rituals began. Day and night, for the next two months, more than 5,000 people went through sealed marriages and other sacred rituals there. The temple was then abandoned—the Mormons now had to move west.

In a letter to the governor of Iowa, Brigham Young wrote, "The time is at hand, in which several thousand free citizens of this great Republic, are to be driven from their peaceful homes and firesides, their property and farms, and their dearest constitutional rights—to wander in the barren plains, and sterile mountains of western wilds . . . or else be exterminated upon their own lands by the peoples, and authorities of the state of Illinois. As life is sweet we have chosen banishment rather than death."

In embarking on this journey into the unknown, the Mormons departed from Parley Street, which led down to the river, from the Seventies Hall along what is now called the Trail of Hope. The sojourners immediately faced the imposing barrier of the Mississippi River. Beginning on February 4, 1846, they crossed the river in small groups by wooden

Opposite page: *The Trail of Hope along which the Mormons traveled on their way westward.*
Above: *A covered wagon on a wooden flatboat that the Mormons used to ferry across the wide Mississippi River.*

ferry, flatboats, and skiffs. These means were slow and awkward, especially in winter—and the violence against the Mormons was increasing. Then, almost miraculously, the wide river froze from bank to bank with a sheet of ice thick enough to support the beleaguered people and their wagons. They could now more easily cross the river.

In his journal, Brigham Young wrote, "The fact is worthy of remembrance that several thousand persons left their homes in midwinter and exposed themselves without shelter, except that afforded by a scanty supply of tents and wagon covers, to a cold which effectually made an ice bridge over the Mississippi River which at Nauvoo is more than a mile

broad. We could have remained sheltered in our homes had it not been for the threats and hostile demonstrations of our enemies, who notwithstanding their solemn agreements had thrown every obstacle in our way, not respecting either life, liberty, or property. . . . Our homes, gardens, orchards, farms, streets, bridges, mills, public halls, magnificent temple, and other public improvements we leave as a living testimony of the falsehood and wickedness of those who charge us with disloyalty to the Constitution of our country, idleness and dishonesty."

On February 16, 1846, the wrenching Mormon exodus across the frozen river began in earnest. Wagons, livestock, and people were backed up for miles, as people waited their turn to cross the ice and head west. John R. Young recalled, "It is the month of February, 1846. The sun is shining brightly, yet the air is keen and cutting. The wheels ring as we drive over the frozen snow. In our home since early morning, all has been hurry and bustle; two wagons stand in our front yard, and my father with two other men, strangers to me, are carrying out our household goods. My mother looks pale, and when I ask her,

Opposite page and above: *In their flight from Nauvoo, the Mormons had to abandon their homes and many of their belongings.*

'What is the matter?' She takes me in her arms, kisses me, and says, 'We are going to leave our home and will never see it again!'"

Others followed through the spring and summer. Only a few people, impoverished or weakened by illness, remained in Nauvoo. However, even this tattered remnant angered the local people. A mob of seven hundred to eight hundred men attacked Nauvoo with small artillery and ordered even the poor and the sick to leave in two hours. On September 17, 1846, the last group of Mormons fled their city beautiful. Thousands of people abandoned the city they had built. Martha Ann Smith, Hyrum and Mary Fielding's daughter, recalled, "I was five years old when we started from Nauvoo. We crossed over the Mississippi in the skiff in the dusk of the evening. We bid goodbye to our dear and old feeble grandmother, Lucy Mack Smith. I can never forget the bitter tears she shed when she bid us goodbye for the last time in her life. She knew it would be the last time she would see her son's family."

Now homeless, 14,000 people had become refugees. The exodus of the Latter-day Saints from their beloved Nauvoo was the largest forced migration in American history. "The Road good, but crooked, following the ridges and passing over a continual succession of hills and hollows," wrote W. Clayton in the first edition of the *Latter-Day Saint's*

Emigrants Guide published in 1848. This guide described every ridge and water hole between Council Bluffs, Iowa, and the valley of the Great Salt Lake in Utah. In 1847, the first group of Mormons had settled here on "land nobody wanted."

In November 1846, an arsonist torched the Nauvoo temple. Three years later, the remainder of the building was struck by a tornado and practically destroyed. People salvaged the blocks of limestone to construct homes and other buildings. Of the Sunstones, only two of the original thirty caps have ever been located. One has been in the Smithsonian Institution since 1989 and the other remains on the original site of the Nauvoo Temple. Encased in a protective housing against rain and sun, this lone Sunstone is a solemn reminder of the enduring spirit of the Mormons.

Many of the brick buildings of Nauvoo remained abandoned until followers of the French philosopher Etienne Cabet came to Nauvoo. Cabet and his followers had to flee France because of hostility toward their utopian beliefs. The Icarians, as they came to be known, first settled in Texas. When they learned that the Mormons had left Nauvoo, the Icarians traveled there in the hopes of buying land and building a society of communal living as Cabet had described in his book, *Voyage en Icarie*. Their group sought to do away

with social classes and poverty by creating a society that provided equally for the basic needs of its citizens. The first group arrived in Nauvoo around 1849. The Icarians bought Temple Square and began their experiment in communal living. They built homes, workshops, and stores. Their school was made of stones from the Mormon Temple.

In 1857, an Icarian named Emile Baxter planted the first grapes for making wine. The French immigrants realized that the soil and climate was similar to the wine regions of their native France. With their German and Swiss neighbors, the Icarians established more vineyards. Soon, there were more than six hundred acres of grapes and the hills of Nauvoo were honeycombed with stone-arched wine cellars. For a few years the commune prospered, but then little disputes flared into bitter rebellion. These conflicts forced Cabet and many followers to move to St. Louis. The rest of the Icarians stayed in Nauvoo until 1860, but then they abandoned the community, too.

Meanwhile, the Mormons became so prosperous and powerful in Utah that the federal officials worried that they had become too independent from the United States. In 1857, President James Buchanan sent an army force, which occupied the territory until 1861. However, under the leadership of Brigham Young, the Mormons made the "desert bloom" within a few years. Families prospered and converts made the long journey to Utah. In 1863, Charles Dickens visited with one group of converts before they sailed for America and observed, "Indeed, I think it would be difficult to find eight hundred people together anywhere else, and find so much beauty and so much strength and capacity for work among them."

After the church renounced plural marriage in 1890, Utah was finally admitted to the statehood in 1896. Governed by a prophet-president and a Council of Twelve Apostles, the church is thriving. Brigham Young University and the Mormon Tabernacle Choir have become widely known and respected institutions.

Although the Church of Jesus Christ of Latter-day Saints and the Reorganized Church of Latter-day Saints, now known as the Community of Christ, have long shared many beliefs, they have never merged. In recent years, they have drifted even further apart. However, in the early 1960s, the two churches joined in a triumphant return of the

Mormons to Nauvoo. Through determination and hard work, they began to restore many of the homes and shops abandoned by their ancestors so long ago. To date, more than three dozen of the original homes and businesses have been restored and are now open to the public.

In April 1999, Gordon Hinckley, president of the Church of Jesus Christ of Latter-day Saints, announced that the Church would rebuild the Nauvoo Temple on the original 3.3-acre site on the Hill in Nauvoo. A groundbreaking ceremony for the 65,000-square-foot building was held in October 1999, and a cornerstone ceremony was held on November 5, 2000. Since the Nauvoo Temple was completed, thousands of people have visited. As with other Mormon temples, the church invited others to visit the temple before the dedication ceremony was held during the last week of June 2002. Now only the faithful who have been baptized and confirmed may enter the temple. Like the original temple, this magnificent building has five stories and a basement. The exterior nearly duplicates that of the original temple.

Today, a three-member First Presidency and the Council of Twelve (Apostles) lead the Church of Jesus Christ of Latter-day Saints. Membership in the United States exceeds 5 million. Founded in 1860, the Reorganized Church of Latter-day Saints, with about 250,000 members, now has its headquarters in Independence, Missouri. The Mormons in both churches continue to believe in revelation and the interdependence of spiritual and temporal life based on the Bible, the Book of Mormon, and revelations to Joseph Smith.

Above: *The Nauvoo Temple columns had Sunstones, like those above, and Starstones on the tops, and Moonstones at the bases.*

With their strong belief in family, community service, education, hard work, thrift, and virtuous living, the Mormons have prospered.

A network of forty thousand LDS missionaries, mostly young volunteers, continue to seek new converts, spreading the church far beyond its "New Zion" in Utah. Mormons from around the world today reverently look upon Nauvoo as a sacred place. Throughout the year, Mormon volunteers from across the United States journey to Nauvoo to reenact everyday pioneer life as it was lived by early Mormon people of the mid-1800s in the little community of Nauvoo. Thousands of Mormons now come to visit the beautiful city, hidden deep in the heart of the country and the souls of the Saints. They regard Nauvoo as the wellspring of their religion as they visit the homes and shops and solemnly walk along the Trail of Hope, recalling the hardships and faith of those who went before them not so long ago.

Above: People come from all over the world to visit present-day Nauvoo.
Opposite page: Overlooking the Mississippi River, the Nauvoo Temple is the most prominent building in the community.

FURTHER READING
AND SOURCES

The following books were consulted in the research and writing of *Nauvoo: Mormon City on the Mississippi River*. The two books by Claudia Lauper Bushman and Richard Lyman Bushman are especially recommended for those who would like to learn more about Nauvoo and the Mormons.

Black, Susan Easton, and William G. Hartley. *The Iowa Mormon Trail: Legacy of Faith and Courage*. Orem, Utah: Helix, 1997.

Black, Susan Easton, and John Telford. *The Nauvoo Temple: Jewel of the Mississippi*. Salt Lake City: Millennial Press, 2002.

Brown, Margie McRae, and Robert Casey. *Nauvoo Restored*. Ogden, Utah: Living Scriptures, 2002.

Bushman, Claudia Lauper, and Richard Lyman Bushman. *Building the Kingdom: A History of Mormons in America*. New York: Oxford University Press, 2001.

Cannon, Janath Russell. *Nauvoo Panorama: Views of Nauvoo Before, During, and After Its Rise, Fall, and Restoration*. Nauvoo, Ill.: Nauvoo Restoration, 1991.

Dickerson, Theodore Earl. *Conflicts Between the Mormons and Non-Mormons: Nauvoo, Illinois, 1839–1846*. Urbana: University of Illinois, 1956.

Flanders, Robert Bruce. *Nauvoo: Kingdom on the Mississippi*. Urbana: University of Illinois Press, 1975.

Givens, George W. *In Old Nauvoo: Everyday Life in the City of Joseph*. Salt Lake City: Deseret Book Co., 1990.

Givens, George W., and Sylvia Givens. *Nauvoo Fact Book: Questions and Answers for Nauvoo Enthusiasts*. Lynchburg, Va.: Parley Street Publishers, 2000.

Hallwas, John E., and Roger D. Launius. *Cultures in Conflict: A Documentary History of the Mormon War in Illinois*. Logan: Utah State University Press, 1995.

———. *Kingdom on the Mississippi Revisited: Nauvoo in Mormon History*. Urbana: University of Illinois Press, 1996.

Holzapfel, Richard Neitzel, and T. Jeffery Cottle. *Old Mormon Nauvoo and Southeastern Iowa: Historic Photographs and Guide*. Santa Ana, Calif.: Fieldbrook Productions, 1991.

Hopkins, Glen S. *Old Nauvoo: Through the Eyes of Artist Glen S. Hopkins*. Mesa, Ariz.: Wandering Minstrel Publishing, 2002.

Jessee, Dean C. *John Taylor: Nauvoo Journal*. Provo: Grandin Book Co., 1996.

Launius, Roger D., and Mark F. McKiernan. *Joseph Smith, Jr.'s Red Brick Store*. Macomb: Western Illinois University, 1985.

Leonard, Glen M. *Nauvoo: A Place of Peace, A People of Promise*. Salt Lake City and Provo: Deseret Book Co.; Brigham Young University Press, 2002.

Madsen, Carol Cornwall. *In Their Own Words: Women and the Story of Nauvoo*. Salt Lake City: Deseret Book Co., 1994.

Miller, David E., and Della S. Miller. *Nauvoo: The City of Joseph*. Bountiful: Utah History Atlas, 1996.

Perkins, Keith W., and Donald Q. Cannon. *Sacred Places: Ohio and Illinois: A Comprehensive Guide to Early LDS Historical Sites*. Salt Lake City: Deseret Book Co., 2002.

Shields, Steven L. *An Illustrated History of Nauvoo*. Independence, Mo.: Herald Publishing House, 1992.

Smith, Joseph, and Paul V. Ludy. *Memories of Old Nauvoo*. Bates City, Mo.: Paul V. Ludy and Associates, 2001.

Swinton, Heidi S. *Sacred Stone: The Temple at Nauvoo*. American Fork, Utah: Covenant Communications, 2002.

Telford, John. *Nauvoo*. Salt Lake City: Eagle Gate, 2002.

Woods, Fred E. *Gathering to Nauvoo*. American Fork, Utah: Covenant Communications, 2002.

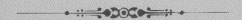

Children's Books

Bushman, Claudia Lauper, and Richard Lyman Bushman. *Mormons in America*. New York: Oxford University Press, 1999.

Robinson, Timothy M., and Robert Barrett. *The Nauvoo Temple Stone*. Salt Lake City: Bookcraft, 2002.